My Story

MARCOS POU GALLO

My Story

MY STORY
By Marcos Pou

Original Title: Mi Historia
Original edition by Guillem Lisicic

https://marcospou.com

17105 Longacres Ln
Odessa, FL 33556

www.humanadventurebooks.com

ISBN: 978-1-941457-35-1

CONTENTS

With José Miguel
in Arizkun

INTRODUCTION

Marcos Pou Gallo was born on September 20, 1991, in Barcelona, into a Catholic family, as the second of six siblings. His childhood and adolescence were those typical of a boy of his time. Marcos's story is an apparently normal one and, at the same time, extraordinary because of how his personal encounter with Christ —which took place at his school— changed his life, through teachers who belonged to the ecclesial movement Communion and Liberation (CL). What captivated him about them was the way they lived their passion for education, for what they taught, for how they treated one another, and for how they accompanied their students in facing the most pressing questions of human existence. By following them, Marcos encountered Christ, and Christ changed his life.

When he began his university studies, he decided to study physics. These were years of intense study, which he soon had to combine with the responsibility —with guidance— of the CL university students' community in Barcelona. Throughout that time, he gathered around him a group of friends who became passionate about life and faith. It was during this university period that he began to take more seriously the possibility of giving his entire life to Jesus in the priesthood.

After finishing his university studies at the age of 23, Marcos entered the Seminary of the Diocese of Barcelona on February 11, 2015, precisely on the day the Church celebrates the feast of Our Lady of Lourdes. On the day he entered, he wrote to some of us:

"Vertigo and total trust, I am Yours, Christ. May this be a path toward holiness. I am happy to give You, my life! That this may prevail over whatever might seem unappealing, over any laziness, or future fatigue. To you, I entrust myself, Mary. Virgin of Lourdes, make me faithful, make me holy!!"

Ten days later, Marcos died in a motorcycle accident.

In the final period of his life, Fr. José Miguel García —a priest who was a father and friend to him, a companion on his journey—suggested that Marcos write about what the God had done in his life so that he might become more aware of how deeply he was loved by Him. In this text, which he himself titled My Story, he recounts his experience as one permeated by the presence of Christ. His words show how he gradually allowed himself to be conquered by the God's tenderness. On the first page he wrote:

"It is somewhat strange to speak of 'my story,' since the only interesting thing in it, the only thing that saves it from being a dull and flat story, is what Christ has done in my life. Therefore, it is really the story of what Christ has done with me."

Those of us who knew Marcos agree that what characterized him most was the vibrant passion with which he lived for Christ, whom he recognized as the center of his entire being and activity, and his urgency to make Him known —hence his missionary zeal. This led him to show affection for everyone he encountered, making others feel welcomed and loved. Every relationship, every meeting, every journey, and even every football match was an opportunity to encounter God and to bear witness to Him to others.

From the recognition of and attraction to his faith in Christ, and from the desire to make it known, the Association of the Faithful Friends of Marcos Pou was born, approved in 2022 by the Archdiocese of Barcelona. We consider Marcos to be a clear example of an ordinary young man who allowed himself to be transformed by Christ, and this transformation beautified him and enabled him to live life to the full. We believe his story is compelling because it shows that living the faith in a reasonable way, and in every area of life, is possible for everyone—also for you, who are about to begin reading this book. In fact, we continue to see how Marcos's life keeps touching the hearts of many who did not know him personally but who, upon discovering his story, awaken in themselves the desire to know Jesus and to live their faith with greater maturity.

Gloria Arcusa
President of the Friends of Marcos Pou Association
marcospou.com

In La Thuile (Italy), during the
CLU summer holidays in 2012

PROLOGUE

Marcos' story is a testimony of life and faith. I accepted the invitation to write this prologue as a gift from God and from Marcos. They have given me the opportunity to share the good that his life has done for many of us.

I was the rector of Tortosa Seminary when I heard the news of his death, about an accident that involved a seminarian from Barcelona. As soon as I learned of his death, I already knew, with an interior clarity, that the Lord had much more to tell us through the life of this young man who, until that moment, was still unknown to me. A seminarian from Tortosa, one of Marcos' classmates, soon confirmed this premonition saying, "Mosén, I hardly knew Marcos, but he had something special."

I read everything that was written about him. In my prayers, I prayed for him. However, I have always felt that he was the one praying for us. What a mystery! I have never seen him, nor have I spoken with him, but my friendship with him is as if I have known him my entire life. What could be the reason for such a deep friendship? Marcos did not live alone. The Truth lived in him. In his life and on his journey to Heaven, he has not left us alone. Living united in the Truth keeps us united with him. Christ is the Truth. And the Truth, as St. John tells us, is Love.

I wanted to know more and more about him. When the book "My Story" fell into my hands, it was like finding a treasure. The writings are a gift from Marcos himself. They allow you to walk alongside him and feel the beating of his heart, the breathing of his soul. I was surprised to see how immense his desire was to seek meaning and the enormous passion with which Marcos lived friendship. Everything in life was a great adventure for him, he wanted to live everything with maximum intensity. The greatest thing Marcos discovered was the living encounter with Christ, the Event that transformed his existence. From that moment on, the joy of faith moved him to live all things with the utmost seriousness and dedication, so that he could live closer to Christ and serve everyone.

I have shared Marcos' testimony, that you now hold in your hands, with many young people. Whenever a difficulty arises during spiritual direction or if there is a need to discern topics like faith, friendship, dating, life in Christ, or vocation, I either refer to the book or give them a copy of "My Story". The outcome has been moving. This book has done so much good for countless young people! They identify with Marcos. What is really incredible, however, is that they not only see him as a light on their path but an example of a Christian life to follow.

In this book, you will discover Marcos' secret: he simply allowed himself to be worked on by God. The Lord shaped him through his friends, educators, family, the poor, and the Church. All of them helped him grow in his intimacy with Christ. For him, being with Christ was as concrete as it was for the disciples. Just a few days before entering seminary Marcos would say, "I am increasingly dominated by a Love, by a face, by a Presence, by Jesus Christ. My life is an adventure and I am happy."

I am sure that this book will be of great help to you. Through Marcos' life you will better understand your own story. All that remains is for us to thank the Lord for having encountered such an authentic witness of the Christian faith. Certainly, the book also has a second half that Marcos will go on narrating in our hearts.

Marcos, your dream of being a priest and living spiritual fatherhood only seemed to have lasted a short time in the eyes of the world— ten days — but that was not the case. God was forming you to Christ throughout your life, and that's why your union with Him came so quickly. We know that your life story was touched by God. We see how you are a light and we experience that you continue to give yourself for all souls, so that we may fall more in love with Christ every day, as the apostles did, as you have done.

+ Javier Vilanova Pellisa
Auxiliary Bishop of Barcelona

MY STORY

CHILDHOOD, WHAT WAS ALWAYS THERE

I was born in 1991 in Barcelona. When I was two years old, we moved to Los Angeles where I lived until I was six. We had some very good years there. When we had to return to Barcelona, one of the things that affected me the most was saying goodbye to the friends we made. I remember asking myself insistently, "Will I see them again? Is there anything that lasts forever?"

When we returned to Barcelona in 1998, my parents enrolled me in a Catholic school where I stayed until I was fifteen. My parents have always been Catholic. They have always loved me a lot and I remember being very happy during my childhood. Even though they were also searching and didn't have everything completely clear, they tried to instill and pass on the faith to me as well. Obviously, I went to Mass with them and repeated what they told me, but I never lived it with much awareness. However, I remember that around the age of twelve, without really knowing why, I started asking my father a lot about the priesthood. I asked about whether all men think about it at some point in their lives and even began to say that I wanted to be a priest. My uncle at that time was also a seminarian. Over time, however, I lost my conviction and curiosity.

The school I went to after living in Los Angeles resembled my parents' way of thinking. It proposed a certain form of Christianity that was formalistic, reduced to habits and customs that weren't attractive to those that came across it. In fact, the more difficult students or simply the ones that questioned the school's rules by acting out were expelled at the first sign of misbehavior. At its core, the school was something of a Catholic bubble, far removed from reality. However in other ways, I remember it as a familiar, pleasant place.

From a very young age, I always felt a great need to be loved and, even more than loved, to be preferred. When team captains chose players on the playground, I always hoped to be one of the first ones picked. Over time, this immense need for affection and preference inevitably got mixed up with the desire to be affirmed, respected, and admired. It motivated me to be a leader, to seek a sense of superiority over others that many times made me think less of them. That was something my brother[1] suffered from many times. Starting in adolescence, all my concern (which lasted for many years afterwards), all my effort, and everything I did was aimed at pleasing, at being part of the group of students who were respected and admired.

I even went so far as to betray my best friends just to be accepted into the "cool" group. However, I also remember being rejected and ignored. I remember that it hurt. I had to constantly reinvent myself to please others. This led me to live in perpetual anxiety, always weary of everything I said or did, and always trying to avoid being excluded. It was suffocating not being able to be myself, not being able to be who I am.

1. Nicolás.

LEAVING THE "BUBBLE"

At sixteen, I changed schools and enrolled at *Abat Oliba*. I left the "bubble" behind and found myself completely surprised by the world around me. I already knew some of my classmates, so it wasn't hard to start school as a new student. On the very first day of class, I found out that practically everyone had lost their virginity and that they all went out late partying at least several times a week.

Changing schools soon turned into an opportunity to be what I wanted to be. A couple of other boys and I quickly became the cool guys in our class, both when it came to partying and making plans with girls. I immediately fell in love with that lifestyle because I finally felt admired. My life revolved around soccer —I played for a year at one of the best clubs in Barcelona— and going out, trying to get with all of the girls I wanted. From then on, my personality gradually changed until I became a teenager who was only interested in himself.

That lifestyle and way of thinking led me to believe that I could and should decide everything by myself. I started to question things at home, especially late-night curfews and getting permission to go out from my parents, or for spending money. The situation at home quickly deteriorated and for almost two years fights around the house became frequent. When my parents set down certain rules, I would always ask "why," and there weren't always reasons. I hated the whole "because I said so" routine. It only encouraged me to start lying like a dog. It got to the point that I was spending nights at friends' houses or even on the train.

Little by little, the world of partying and constantly making plans started to consume me. I dedicated all of my time to it, even though I never really enjoyed that way of having fun. Drugs, for example, were never attractive to me. My parents, despite all their frustration (and looking back, I've come to see just how much they loved me), never gave in. They continued to raise me by example and saved me from getting too involved in that scene. Without a doubt, it was a tremendous act of love that the Lord chose my family specifically for me. I have never lacked affection at home. That affection saved me from taking refuge in marijuana like my friends did. Or the idea of sleeping with a different girl every other night: it just didn't sit right with me.

With his brothers, on the day of Juan and Mateo's First Communion

RELATIONSHIPS WITH GIRLS

My relationship with girls was always a source of pain and discomfort for me. Miraculously, I never slept with any of them. I always justified myself to my friends by saying I was waiting for the right one. It was very hard for me to look at the ones I treated badly. I was overwhelmed by shame and pain. All the friendships I had with girls always withered away. I felt a tremendous powerlessness not knowing how to treat them well or how to see them for who they were. Now it is clear to me that the desire to treat women purely and to look at them in the right way isn't something I made up, it was always there.

I remember one time, a Saturday afternoon when I was bored at home, I messaged Marta, an ex-girlfriend, trying to win her back (with ex-girlfriends, somehow it was always easier). She told me she was nearby, at a friend's house who wouldn't be back until later...so I went. After a while together, suddenly her friend called to say she was on her way, and Marta rushed to get me out of the house. I remember walking out the door and turning to say goodbye and finding it already closed. That's when I realized I wasn't meant to treat women that way. Immediately, I was overwhelmed with anger towards her for using me like that, but I also realized I had treated her the same way. An intuition kept circling around in my head, "I am not meant to treat others like this, nor to be treated this way."

FAITH ISN'T INTERESTING

I lived life the way my parents raised me to, but over time, I lost interest in going to Mass on Sundays (I would lie saying I had gone) and began to question many of our faith traditions. Suddenly, the God I had mechanically prayed to all my life, the one who only told me what I had to do, lost significance.

Soon the disenchantment I was experiencing with the Church began to permeate everything in my life. Very few things truly excited me. Sooner or later, in everything I experienced, I felt a sense of disillusionment; everything disappointed me, and over time it became a burden. As a result, I never fully committed myself to anything—neither to friendships, nor to sports, nor to my studies. My life was dominated by an enormous boredom that I only occasionally managed to "overcome."

THE MYSTERY

I never stopped believing that there was something more, never. Even though I stopped living my faith, there was always a small part of me convinced that there was something more. Not only that, but I've also always felt a deep need to connect with that mysterious "point" that I somehow always intuited existed. I remember countless times when I tried to enter more deeply into that "point of mystery". Back then I conceived of it in an abstract, emotional, or sentimental way. I remember escaping alone many afternoons to watch the sunset with a beer and a good book, or I recall enjoying music that stirred a kind of nostalgia in me, spending hours listening to those songs. I remember enjoying serious conversations where these same topics came up (like destiny). I even remember, when my brother and I went surfing, listening to the silence of the sea and gazing out past the horizon. Those kinds of things always stirred something deep within me. Certain things in the world gave me the sense that something was hidden in what we see, but I didn't really know what it was or how to get to know it better. And always, always, always, there was a trace of nostalgia in me, especially at night. I always wondered who would heal that nostalgia, who would arrive and embrace me at night with tenderness. In fact, when I read fantasy novels like "The Hobbit" or watched movies like 'The Lord of the Rings," the following thought came to mind, "These people live a life full of real adventure, can mine be like that too?"

I've always had questions that caused me great anxiety, usually about death or existence. Like, "What if I didn't exist? What if everything ends? What if I'm wasting my time?" Urgent questions that I had to stop thinking about because they kept me awake at night.

This mysterious "point" made me live with a special sensitivity towards the things I did or enjoyed, like music or film, approaching them in a more profound way. Beautiful landscapes and being in nature are things that I enjoyed a lot. They made me feel that something was missing within me, something I couldn't recognize.

SOMETHING STARTS TO HAPPEN IN HIGH SCHOOL

After the first few months at my new school, some teachers began to attract my attention. They were true educators, capable of engaging students and getting them excited about what they were studying. Classes became more intense and a great curiosity awoke in me, especially for History and Physics

These teachers started to have a huge effect on me. Even the language they used was provocative. They spoke about desire, happiness, expectation, sadness, and questions about what it means to be alive. I had never heard anyone talk about my humanity like that before. Soon, in a simple way, I began to enjoy their manner of speaking, teaching, and interacting with each other. The word happiness, for example, fascinated me. It seemed to me to be something greater than just "being happy" or "feeling good," phrases I used all the time. These questions began to nag at me day and night, and they started to raise many other questions within me. I realized I had never thought about my destiny, what I truly wanted, what made me happy. I realized that, at sixteen years old, I was already a jaded old man.

Moreover, some of them, like me, showed a special sensitivity toward certain things—such as going to the mountains, the sea, classical music, or cinema—and I enjoyed (even if I didn't have things clear) talking about man, about happiness, about the great questions of life.

The subject I liked least was Catalan, but I found out that the teacher, Suca[1], knew a great deal about cinema, and I began to approach him at the end of classes. He was always a spur for me; he saw something in me that no one else had seen—the possibility of a change, of an awakening. He constantly challenged me in the same way: about mediocrity. He challenged me to recognize whether my life was a true adventure, or rather something mediocre.

Movies have always been a passion of mine (for a while I even had a movie blog). Over time I also developed a taste for older, less well known, but good films. Finding an interesting teacher who shared that same restlessness thrilled me. Little by little we began to exchange films. Afterwards we would meet and exchange a few words about the one we had watched. When we would analyze the films together, I always tried to match his level of observation, talking about the script, the performances, the technical approach, or the director. It was clear that he knew much more than I did about film. However, what fascinated me the most was his surprising ability to delve into the meaning of things and decipher the message of the films. He perceived the deeper meaning of the films we discussed much better than me. He would say to me, "Yes, everything you're saying is true, but what is the director trying to tell us?" Once he lent me the movie "Citizen Kane" (which is about a rich man who achieves everything in life). After finishing the movie, I sent him a message asking, "Yes, it's good, but why?". He replied, "Because a man can conquer the world, but still lose himself." No one had ever summed up my life as well and as quickly as Suca did in that moment.

I remember going to the cinema to see "Copying Beethoven" and leaving there in awe. I immediately got hooked on his *Ninth Symphony*, spending hours and hours listening to it and thinking about what Suca told us about Romanticism and a poet named Giacomo Leopardi. In class, Suca would always read us poetry by Leopardi, a Romantic writer. One he often read to us was this:

1. Josep Maria Sucarrats Vilà, was the Catalan Language and Literature teacher at the high school. Due to their friendship, Marcos called him by the nickname Suca, a shortened version of his last name.

> *The inability to be satisfied with anything earthly, or, so to speak, with the whole earth; to consider the incalculable vastness of space, the number and marvelous mass of worlds, and to find everything too little and small for the capacity of one's own mind; to imagine the number of infinite worlds, and the infinite universe, and always to accuse things of their insufficiency and their nothingness, and to suffer want and emptiness, and yet boredom, seems to me the greatest sign of greatness and nobility that can be seen in human nature*[2].

Because of my friendship with Suca, I started to hang out with a small group of teachers and students who used to meet twice a week. I soon made friends with other teachers as well. I was surprised by the closeness they treated us with and the camaraderie between them. I also began to take an interest in the other students who met with them and started to attend what they called "School of Community"[3]. During this weekly meeting of teachers and students, they would talk about life and read from Fr. Luigi Giussani[4]. The life of this specific priest became very appealing to me. The desire for things not to be fleeting but to last forever, something I had always wanted, was consciously welcomed and nurtured within the group. Although I didn't always attend regularly and sometimes didn't even go at all, I did start going to some of the events they hosted and talking sporadically with others that attended the School of Community, like Miquel Casajuana, Luis Seguí, and Ferrán Riera (some of the teachers that belonged to Communion and Liberation, known as CL).

2. Giacomo Leopardi, "Thoughts", in Poetry and Prose, Alfaguara, Madrid 1990, pp. 465–466

3. Weekly catechetical meeting of the members of Communion and Liberation

4. Milanese priest (1922–2005), founder of the ecclesial movement Communion and Liberation.

MY FAMILY SEES A CHANGE

In parallel, both my uncle Íñigo and my cousin Rafa—who was a seminarian at the time—began to see something awakening in me. We made an effort to meet in person and exchange emails regularly, to talk about ourselves and our faith. They accompanied me on my journey toward seminary from the very beginning. Both of them lived an intense life of faith. Íñigo in Opus Dei and Rafa with the Legionaries of Christ. Over time, my cousin Rafa started encouraging me to participate in different activities with the Legionaries of Christ. I went on "missions" with them two years in a row, an important part of their charism.

Those were somewhat confusing times for me. As I became more interested in my faith, what was awakening in me was still very weak. The time I spent with the Legionaries left me unsatisfied. Something was missing. One thing that was difficult for me, for example, was prayer. I often asked myself, "Who am I supposed to be talking to? Should I convince myself that there's a God listening to me, does He even exist?" That kind of doubt troubled me. Even so, my relationships with my uncle and cousin kept me from distancing myself any further from the Church. I made good friendships with other people through them, which encouraged me to continue living my faith life. It was also helpful to meet people my age who questioned certain things but still lived their faith without giving up anything or changing in any substantial way. It wasn't long before I realized the enormous duality that those I had met were living: they lived part of their lives doing as they pleased, and their faith life was separate.

This confused me about where I stood in life. With time, my life was divided: I fell into my previous lifestyle, I went to CL events, and activities put on by other lay communities. Nonetheless, what I had seen wasn't really changing me. I didn't belong or follow one group, and as a result, everything remained at a surface level. I remember, for example, going for two years to the CL high school vacation in Picos de Europa, and to missions for two years, and they didn't change anything in me. Thanks be to God, Suca never let me completely disconnect, and Luis Seguí[1] kept provoking me in class.

1. Luis Seguí Pons, Director of the Abat Oliba Loreto School, 2002–2010.

SOMETHING AWAKENS

During that period in my life, my relationship with Rafa awakened within me something that had been dormant for a long time: my vocation. In our conversations, the topic began to come up, and the question about my vocation and the possibility of becoming a priest resurfaced.

As time wore on, I started thinking about it more and more, however only two years later, that chapter was closed again. Around that same time, Rafa had suggested taking the call seriously and proposed a certain path to verify it. But shortly thereafter, just before I was about to go in that direction, someone at school told me that, for those graduating high school, CL proposed a pilgrimage to Our Lady of Częstochowa, and that the focus of the pilgrimage was centered around vocation. In reality, it wasn't focused on the vocation I had in mind. Even so, upon hearing that, I understood that I had to go. It was all rather mysterious, but I thought, "Perfect, this will help me discover what I have to do." It was interesting to realize that I actually didn't have the faintest idea about vocation, that vocation isn't just about making some life decision. During the pilgrimage, I said to the Virgin Mother, "Okay, I'll wait, you tell me." After that, the idea of my vocation went dormant again.

XVII
CSIC
NIKE

LIFE OUT THERE ISN'T WHAT IT USED TO BE

During my third year of high school, I sort of resumed the life I was living before. Truthfully, I had never completely abandoned it. But I began to find myself sad and apathetic. Largely due to the influence of a few friends, I spent less and less time with people from the movement[1]. I shrank back into my old habits, wanting less, settling for less, and living a life that was increasingly full of distraction.

Curiously, getting to know the lay movement of Communion and Liberation (CL) made me "unhappy." Let me explain. CL awakened a desire in me, a restlessness that nothing could fully satisfy or quench. It led me to realize how sad the life I had been living was, how empty it was, how everything seemed to be withering away. Little by little, I discovered that if I didn't get more involved with CL, that is, if I didn't start living my life with them, that I wouldn't just be unhappy, I would become even more unhappy than I was before. The point is, once you've discovered how you want to live, living for less isn't worth it. CL had left an indelible mark on my experience. When I was with them it was impossible not to think about the point of friendship, or camaraderie, or what life meant in general. Abandoning that experience was a real loss, it was a diminished sense of living.

1. Movement of Communion and Liberation.

In Pamplona with Ignacio,
José Miguel, and Daniel

MY ENCOUNTER WITH HIM

At the end of the year, I attended school of community with CL a bit more often, thanks to Suca, who was always taking me along. Even though I didn't understand anything, I decided to go back to the Picos summer camps. It was my third time going. That year, I met Dani Cerrillo. He was a regular in the movement, and a beautiful friendship developed between us. That year, I also met Edu Germán.

Picos was a time in my life when I could rest, a moment when I could live without worrying about what others thought of me. I was treated well for who I was. However, at the same time, I really didn't make much of an effort to take seriously what was said or proposed to me. That year in Picos, I understood many things about myself, like why I suffered so much in my interactions with women. A priest named Pancho helped me figure it out. He explained to me that I was separating physical interactions from affection and that I was conceiving of relationships with women in a purely instinctive way. He made me realize that kissing a girl is telling her that you love her, and if that's not true, it's a lie. Thanks to insights like this, I began to desire and pray to treat women better. It was there that I started to have friends—real friends—like Elena from Córdoba, with whom I still remain close with to this day.

At Picos, they put Dani, Edu, and another guy they call Malote in the same tent with me. One of those nights, the four of us stayed up talking. Edu had to leave the next day without finishing the camp. I remember he wanted us to talk about what those days had meant to him. Amazed, he told us about what he had experienced. He began to share what he desired, what had always been missing in his life, and what had happened to him during those days. I listened closely, and even though I can't recall a single word he said, what I do know is that my heart stopped. I was left speechless and found myself thinking, "What's happening? I don't know, but this is for me—this is happening to me!" In my friend's experience, in the way he spoke about himself, I recognized myself. He talked about who I was in a way no one ever had. I found what I had always been searching and waiting for, even though I had never fully understood what I was looking for myself.

No one had ever spoken about me in that way. That night, I finally found what I had always sensed and needed but had never seen. Even now, I'm still discovering what happened that night, but it's the same experience as the Samaritan woman who met Jesus at the well, "He told me everything I have ever done."[1] I also recognize myself in what Fr. Giussani says about the encounter with Jesus, quoting Mario Victorino, "When I met Christ, I discovered myself a man."[2]

Due to the overwhelming nature of what happened that night, an enormous silence came over me. The encounter I had was with something bigger than Edu or any of us four. Someone had used Edu to reach me that night. The rest of my life has consisted solely of getting to know that "Someone" who was speaking to me. Nothing since that moment has ever been the same. I have never been able to deny or to convince myself that what I met that night was an illusion—it was something that corresponded completely with what I desire and hope for even now.

1. Jn 4,5–43.

2. Mario Victorino, "In epistola ad Ephesios," Book II, in Marii Victorini Opera Exegetica, Chapter 4, Verse 14: "Cum cognoscimus Christum, viri efficimur."

The next morning, when I woke up, I looked out toward the mountains and thought, "I don't quite know what happened, what all this means… But God, that mysterious 'point' that had never entered my life, has entered, has become tangible." This was my encounter with Christ.

Little by little, I began to recognize myself in everything the people from CL were saying. They were speaking about my experience too. Despite still having doubts or not understanding everything, I became more open toward what they said or proposed. Everything changed. The order of priorities in my life began to shift dramatically. I started to—now truly—always be with my friends from CL. I even chose a different major for college from the one I had planned to study. I had always thought about studying Telecommunications Engineering because many people talked about the job opportunities or the money. The truth is, however, I always liked physics more. In physics there was a creative intelligence behind things, and objectively, I enjoyed it more. The criteria I used up until then—ensuring a bright future or money—gave way to another, "Where is God calling me?" Thanks to my high school physics teacher, Ferrán Riera, I understood that I should choose physics in college.

MY PARENTS AND CL

My parents, especially my mother, began to take an interest in what was happening to me and came to my school to meet Luis Seguí. I remember that we would have dinner at his house and ours every so often. They were incredibly interesting dinners where Luis introduced us to an appreciation for wine, whiskey, fine cigars, and constantly told us stories about his friends from CL. He told us about extraordinary things that moved us deeply and left us speechless. He told us about people with incredible lives (like the ones he brought to the school's "school for parents"[1]) or phrases and anecdotes from Giussani. It was unprecedented that I could drink at home with my parents or that we could share our questions and interests so freely over dinner. Those meals as a family were an event that captivated all of us. From then on, my parents grew closer to CL and embarked on a beautiful journey. I remember hearing my mother crying, "I didn't know that God is love." For me, it has been one of the most beautiful gifts the Lord has given me in my life to be able to walk the path of faith and discover CL at the same time as my parents. It was thrilling (and still is today) to discover together what the Lord placed before us and to live this journey in such an intimate way, witnessing how they grew and changed. That has been, and still is, a gift. Little by

1. During the 2006–2010 academic years, Abat Oliba School promoted monthly conferences with various guest speakers to address and discuss topics of a diverse nature, particularly education and culture. "school for parents" was initially aimed at the parents of students and teachers, but after just a few months, given the large number of participants and the success of the lectures, it was opened up to the rest of the educational community.

little, it radically transformed our family life and the way we lived with and accompanied each other, reminding and challenging one another on the latest discussions we had with Luis, and marveling together at what we were discovering about CL. It was from that moment that my uncle Yago and some of my aunts began to draw closer to CL as well, making us all witnesses to a beautiful story.

It was then that I started to fully engage with CL. The summer after I finished school, I signed up not only for Picos and Częstochowa but also for the *Rimini Meeting*[2], where I met many of my friends, like Gigi.

I began to discover an entire world in which faith was lived as an adventure, something reasonable that changed the way I looked at everything.

2. A week-long cultural event held at the fairgrounds in the city of Rimini (Italy) that has been organized every August since 1980, by the "Meeting for Friendship Among Peoples" Association. The Meeting features a wide range of conferences, debates, concerts, roundtables, and discussions on topics related to culture, religion, politics, economics, and art.

Party with friends from the
Loreto Abat Oliba School

MY TIME IN CLU

Following that summer[1], I joined the CLU (Communion and Liberation University Students) and started participating in all the different proposals they organized. My first year of university was a confusing one. I attended the School of Community and participated in charitable work[2] with Bocatas[3], but it didn't feel like I was having the experience people talked about. I gladly repeated many of the things that were said, but always with a hint of doubt. I recognized that what was said at the School of Community and my own thoughts were similar, but I also perceived an immense distance from what was being said and my own life. I was confused and couldn't quite see how to bridge that gap, how I could embark on the path being set out before me.

1. 2008–2009 Academic Year

2. With the spiritual and human maturation of its members in mind, Communion and Liberation encourages both young people and adults to freely and gratuitously dedicate their time to missionary work with the needy, specifically through a commitment to some form of charitable activity.

3. "Bocatas" is a non-profit association that was founded in Barcelona in May 2007. Still active to this day, its members dedicate Friday afternoons to providing psychosocial support to marginalized people suffering from addiction to drugs and alcohol, especially in Barcelona's Raval neighborhood.

Vacation in the Aran Valley
with José Miguel García

FRIENDS FROM CLU

It was also difficult to make good friends. I worried too much about pleasing or befriending people that seemed more interesting and popular, and I never met anyone that was a true companion on the journey of life. It was the same with university. I followed certain subjects with a lot of enthusiasm, but I neglected studying and didn't fully engage. Little by little, my excitement for university faded. It started to seem impossible to really verify my faith in the way we used to talk about it.

SUMMER PLANS

That summer the proposal for CLU was to go on the *Camino de Santiago* on pilgrimage together (it was a holy year)[1]. Throughout the pilgrimage, we worked daily on a text by Julián Carrón[2] that continually repeated, "Don't expect a miracle, expect a journey."[3] César Senra came one day to give a talk about his life. I was struck by the loyalty he had to his heart, that he was unafraid to acknowledge the moments in his life when he had lived a lie.

It was painful for me to discover that everything I had said and done throughout the year was empty. I couldn't identify a single moment in which I had recognized Christ during that year. I realized that I would have gladly lived the way they were talking about, but that it hadn't been that way for me that year. So, I committed myself to praying day after day, "Lord, may I come to know You, as much as the disciples knew You; help me to get back on the path." It was then that I began to form friendships with those who started to become my true friends, and who, curiously, weren't the ones I had chosen throughout the year, like the friendship that emerged with Monsignor Miguel Ramón (a priest

1. 2010

2. Fr. Julián Carrón Pérez, diocesan priest and president of the Fraternity of Communion and Liberation from 2005 to 2021.

3. Translated from: Julián Carrón Pérez, "Esperaos un camino, no un milagro. Mensaje con motivo de la Peregrinación Macerata-Loreto," https://espanol.clonline.org/noticias/iglesia/2011/06/13/esperaos-un-camino-no-un-milagro.

from Barcelona), or with Pep Albín, who took very good care of me during that time of my life.

The pilgrimage did me a lot of good and when I got back home, I went with my family to Tortosa. Some CL (Communion and Liberation) families from Madrid had organized a vacation there together. It was the first time that my parents attended an event like that and also the first one we went on as a whole family. My brother[4] also started to get closer to CL around that time. It was a discovery for all of us. Seeing how those families lived together, how parents and children treated each other, and how they sang surprised us. I was fascinated by what happened during those days, especially within my own family. Seeing my parents open their hearts to the people they met there and the way they did it deeply moved me. Something was happening right before my eyes. Moreover, that's where I met Betty (a Memores Domini)[5] who is now one of my best Friends. She helped me a lot. The profound friendship that emerged in just a few days with her and Miguel Ramón left their mark on me. I remember heading home and being in awe, thinking, "Who are You who makes this happen right here before me?"

I couldn't take my eyes away from certain things that happened while I was with that group of people. Amazement at what had happened during those days prevailed in me, and above all, I felt an urgent need to understand who was giving all of it to me, how I could get to know Him better. What happened with my parents seemed unthinkable to me. It's extraordinary that a person can change and become passionate again about who they are and what things are.

4. Nicolás.

5. The Memores Domini are a private, universal ecclesial association whose members live and engage in their apostolate through the world of work, with total dedication to God. Don Luigi Giussani founded the association in 1964, and it was recognized by the Holy See in 1988.

ROCÍO

I fell in love with Rocío while we were in Tortosa. She would later become my girlfriend. I already knew her from Picos and Częstochowa, but we had never really interacted until that summer when we ended up on several trips together. Although we didn't talk much during Picos or the other places where our paths crossed, I remember that whenever I looked at her a thought kept circling in my mind, "This girl will be important." Little by little, we started talking more and more, and I began sharing the things happening in my life. It so happened that her parents and mine had become very close friends in Tortosa, so we saw each other again shortly after the school year started.

The urge to tell her that I had fallen in love with her eventually became overwhelming. It was very hard for me to say it, although the truth is that (like all women) she had sensed it for a while. Finding out that she was still somehow in love with her ex-boyfriend made me feel terrible, but for the first time in my life, I wanted to love her even if her feelings for me weren't reciprocal. After spending an entire weekend in Madrid with my family at her house, I didn't have the courage to confess my feelings. However, the following weekend I couldn't hold it back any longer and I went to see her just to tell her. I was moved by the way she looked at me. She told me that she wasn't in love with me.

As time went on, we talked more and more. Soon we were speaking every day, sharing everything that was happening in our lives. I began to notice that she was also becoming interested in me. One weekend, she told me she had something important to share. One of the people who had been important in her life, Franco Nembrini[1], was coming to spend a few days in Madrid, and she said she needed to tell me about the conversation she had with him. In my mind, I was already celebrating.

1. Founder and former director of La Traccia school in Bergamo (Italy).

A NEW DEVELOPMENT IN MY RELATIONSHIPS AND THE REUNION

In October[1], during the Pope's visit to the Sagrada Familia[2], Rocío came to Barcelona and we went out to eat. That day, she admitted that she had fallen in love with me, but she also said she was worried. The pain from her last relationship was still fresh, and she told me that being in love didn't seem like enough to her—she needed to discern whether starting a relationship together aligned not only with our own desires but also with God's will. She said she wanted to entrust our relationship to Christ, and for that, she proposed that we keep our distance (without talking) for a while. The idea was to place what was happening between us in God's hands and, above all, to learn that the other person isn't ours, that we don't possess their destiny.

That day was a gift for me. Until that day, falling in love with a girl or dealing with one had never had anything to do with my destiny. Rocío brought into my life one of the greatest things I have ever discovered, the impact of faith on life and the importance of faith in relationships. From then on, I began to discover how faith changes life, making everything more human. Even courtship. That's why I accepted her proposal. Despite there being a lot that I didn't understand, something propelled me forward with

1. Marcos is referring to the month of November of that same year.

2. Pope Benedict XVI made an apostolic visit to Spain and visited Santiago de Compostela and Barcelona (November 6–7, 2010). Sunday, November 7th, he celebrated Mass in the basilica of the Sagrada Familia and consecrated the church and altar.

excitement. I sensed that with this approach, we were loving each other in a truer way.

She suggested that we go three months without talking. The first few weeks, I was happy about it and grateful, but over time I started to doubt the decision and to struggle. Two things terrified me: the first, that we might fall out of love; the second, that I might fail to seize the immense opportunity God was giving me to grow and not discover everything Rocío had spoken to me about. It seemed like Christ had given me a tremendous chance to treat the girl I loved the way I had always wanted. In other words, He was giving me a precious opportunity to educate myself.

The fear that either she or I may fall out of love was provocative. I remember talking about it with Malote, and he told me, "Don't forget that she is not your destiny." But I didn't understand, and as time went by (always respecting the distance she asked from me), I began to suffer. I decided to write to her about what was happening to me, and she responded in a very serious way, saying: "This time is for discovering Christ."

After a month had passed and Christmas was over, I began telling my friends about what I was going through. Over the course of a week, I had dinner and lunch with each of them, sharing my confusion and what was causing me to suffer. All of them, in their own way, tried to help me. Then one Friday, after lunch, while clearing the dishes, I told one of my best friends, Jordi. We were in the kitchen, and I explained how bad I felt, that I wasn't doing what Rocío had told me. Then, through him, I recognized the same gaze that had captivated me in Picos. That same silence that had filled me in the tent washed over me again and a thought struck me: "I know this gaze." I recognized the same face I had encountered in Picos, that "Someone" with an unmistakable way of being who filled my heart. Through Jordi, but not entirely because of Jordi himself, a gaze of infinite tenderness said to me, "Why are you so distressed when I love you?" That day, I could breathe again. I let go of all the weight I had placed on myself, and I discovered in a very real way that Christ loved me and was real in my life.

If I look back, I can't help but recognize that I had the same experience as the disciples, exactly the same. The Gospels speak of a real and tangible encounter with a person of flesh-and-blood who had an exceptional way of looking at others. In my case, it was the same, but through a specific person. In a mysterious way, through Jordi, I discovered and touched Christ. It's a mysterious experience, yet at the same time very simple. I recognized a unique face of love that came to meet me. The encounter with Christ that I had in Picos became a little clearer.

I remember leaving that house like the disciples walking to Emmaus, "Did our hearts not burn within us while we listened to Him speak?[3]" That's the experience the Lord was calling me to through this distance—to seek in Christ, and not in Rocío, the fulfillment of my life. And mysteriously, living this way didn't diminish my love for her; rather, it increased it.

When the time for separation was over, I went to Madrid happy about what had happened. I was able to tell Rocío that yes, I had discovered Christ during that time, and that this made me capable of looking at her as something that wasn't mine, as someone I could accept into my life if God willed it. Alfonso, her friend, helped me a lot during that period and later supported us tremendously. We started going out that same day, and I stayed in Madrid for a whole week.

Those were beautiful days. I was deeply moved by how we treated each other. But what surprises me the most, even now, is that it only took two days for Rocío's heart and mine to leap up and out. Our hearts were complaining about something. An alarm bell went off inside of us when we were alone. It's true that we had been waiting to see each other for a long time, but even that wasn't enough—nor was being with the person I loved enough. We had

3. Lk 24,32.

come to know who truly fulfilled us: Christ. And from the depths of our hearts, a thought emerged, "If being with her isn't connected to Him, it won't be enough." After finding the courage to talk about it together (any other girl might have gotten upset for not "being enough"), we discovered that we were called to live with the distance and respect that this time had generated and helped us to experience. From the very first day, my relationship with Rocío was always immersed in this small distance that helped us recognize that the other doesn't belong to you.

That year university life was an adventure. Studying with my classmates became interesting—like when I met Adrián, for example. At one point I organized a barbecue at the university to raise money for Japan after an earthquake[4]. What happened to one of the girls during the barbecue, something which she spoke about later during a CL university assembly, was beautiful. Basically, she had to let go of certain prejudices she had about me and started coming to Bocatas (our charitable activity). Also Pep asked me that year to participate in the Diaconia[5], and even though the little group was going through a difficult moment it was a gift to be involved at all. Little by little, I started engaging more within the School of Community and it became a fundamental part of my life. Gradually, I started comparing what I was living in my life more and more with what we were reading and discussing. When Españita asked me to lead the School of Community with him, the responsibility it demanded only deepened this work of self-reflection.

4. On March 11, 2011 there was a magnitude 9 earthquake on the Richter scale that ravaged the Japanese coasts. There were almost sixteen thousand deaths and three thousand went missing.

5. Group of university students that help the responsible of CLU in their work of service to the community.

SADNESS AND NOSTALGIA

Throughout that year (and deep down it had always been this way for her), Rocío suffered a great sadness. She always spoke to me about it. A sadness, a kind of immense nostalgia, invaded everything she experienced, absolutely everything. It was around that time that I discovered Rocío had the most beautiful heart I'd ever known in my life. I've never seen anything like it, nothing compares. No one else I have ever met has a heart so clearly defined by always wanting more, needing to be loved and accompanied in everything. The loyalty she had to her heart and her constant restlessness began to change me and make me a participant in that way of living life. Over time, I started to become more loyal to my own heart and to what made it beat. It was a beautiful thing to share everything that was happening to us with total loyalty and sincerity.

During that period, it so happened that Fr. Carrón began speaking to us a lot about the heart, about sadness, and the nostalgia for something we struggle to identify: something we call the religious sense. It was then that School of Community started to become fascinating, something that helped us understand ourselves and what was happening to Rocío and I. Above all, one phrase from Dostoevsky became like a companion for her, "That eternal and holy sadness which certain chosen souls, once they have tasted and known it, would never exchange for cheap satisfaction[1]." Without a doubt, she affected the heart I have now, or perhaps

1. Fiódor Mijáilovich Dostoievski, "The Demons," in Complete Works, vol. II, Madrid: Aguilar 1986, p. 1098.

she awakened it. She awakened in me a tremendous desire, and since then, many nights I also suffer that anguish, that immense nostalgia that reminds me of just how much I need Christ.

All of this has allowed me to walk a beautiful path. I am starting to discover to what extent Giussani is right when he says that everything in us is pure need, an adventure that changes life. By getting to know ourselves, we begin to understand what happens to us in life and come to know the One who made us this way. To put it another way, this desire helps us understand what we need and where to look for it. I'll share a very simple example that, for me, was very vivid. I remember one day I went to the hospital because of a pain in my leg. As I was leaving the hospital, I kept checking my phone to see if there were any messages, something as simple as, "Did it go well?"—an affectionate message showing that someone cared about me. I remember thinking of Rocío and saying to myself, "I'd be thrilled to get a message from her asking how it went." Surprised by this thought, an idea struck me, "If all I need is this, whether it happens or not, I'll still be sad. But if deep down it becomes a sign of a higher need and I ask for it from the Only One who can truly give it to me, then it's different." Little by little, my heart has become the Lord's preferred place to get my attention—it's His way of warning me and reminding me that I need Him.

With Rocío on vacation in Masella

GARCI, YAGO AND THE AWAKENING OF MY VOCATION

That same year[1], I met the man who has become a father, José Miguel. At the Bocatas party that year—I don't quite remember why—I approached him and greeted him. Without really knowing why, I told him that deep down I had always had a question about my vocation, but that little by little it had faded. With a very serious expression on his face He said to me, "That's not something you should neglect." I immediately got scared and asked him, "So, what do I do to take care of it?" He told me to pray to the Virgin Mary and ask for two things (which I've always done since then), "Help me clarify my vocation, and help me love it." That same day, with very little thought, I mentioned it to Rocío. This upset her, so I asked that we never talk about it again. It was admirable on her part that she never brought it up again, even though I'm sure there were moments when she knew it was still at the forefront of my thoughts. From then on, I started handling it more discreetly (something I've never been good at), and eventually I tried to live it in intimacy with Christ and with patience.

Throughout that year, my relationship with my uncle Yago grew tremendously and he started to become one of the people who accompanied me the most. He was a parish priest in Benicasim. That year I began spending more time with him and with the community that was emerging in his parish. I've always felt connected to that community and felt the need to bear witness

1. 2011

to their journey. And so Rocío and I decided to spend a few days there with my uncle and the others. Those were beautiful days in our relationship, and we really enjoyed ourselves with the married couples we met from CL. But somehow—and it started there—I felt a sharp pain in my chest when I was with Rocío. I found our relationship extraordinary, I loved her deeply, but something inside me hurt. This was especially the case when people joked or made comments about our future. Something inside me wasn't certain. However, despite that, I still loved her very much.

When she returned to Madrid, I stayed behind and spent a few days with my uncle, sharing in the life he led. I fell in love with his life: with his fatherhood, with his way of accompanying others, with the interactions among the priests there (with whom I also became friends), and with so many other things. Most importantly, I began to pray the Liturgy of the Hours regularly. I was excited by the idea that the Lord would dominate my entire day. I was called to live that way. I was fascinated by the idea that Christ wouldn't just be present in isolated moments of my life, but define the entire day. I discovered this through my uncle, by observing his life of prayer and dedication to God.

CALCUTTA AND WORLD YOUTH DAY (WYD)

That summer, I went to Calcutta with my uncle and a really great group of his students. The days were intense, during which I learned to work without thinking about myself (in volunteering, it's easy to fall into that trap) and took on the most difficult or least appealing tasks. Even so, I realized how strong my tendency was to think of myself, to affirm myself. I especially noticed it in my interactions with others. However, the work we did in those houses introduced me to another possibility for life, namely offering up all that I did for the work of Another.

There are two things I should highlight from that trip. First, meeting Sister María Ruah. She's a Spanish nun who lives in Asansol at the leper colony, where a few of us worked for a week. She was a beautiful witness of life, joy, and dedication, but above all of what it means to have a relationship with God. She spoke of Christ as her husband. At times, it felt as if she could touch Him, as if He were truly there. I'll never forget her response when I asked her how to have a faith like hers, "You already know, Marcos—prayer and dialogue in everything you do." Since then, I've sought and constantly nurtured my own dialogue with Christ in all aspects of my life. Second, my vocation. Many people approached me asking about it during the trip. Both the sisters and laypeople hinted that I seemed like a priest. At times, it felt like there was a bit of an agenda to "convince" me that I should be a priest, and it became hard for me to discern when it was the Lord speaking to me and when it was someone projecting their own plan onto God's, telling me what I should do. That troubled me and made me nervous.

After returning from Calcutta, I went to World Youth Day (WYD)[1]. Those were also beautiful days, albeit exhausting. Once again, the possibility arose, as a volunteer, to give my life for Another—something I didn't do often enough. Suddenly, being around Rocío became more painful, and at times I avoided her, not understanding what was happening. The topic of vocation was still making me nervous, so I wrote to Garci again, asking to discuss it calmly. Two days earlier, the Pope had said to seminarians, "Only those who are certain should become priests."[2] Garci reassured me greatly and recommended that I focus on three things. First, the sacraments. Second, a relationship with Rocío that was completely open to the Lord's will. Third, exercising fatherhood with my friends. It's curious that, shortly afterward, Nacho Carbajosa[3] suggested I take on the role of CLU (Communion and Liberation University) leader in Barcelona. I always saw that role tied to Garci's presence as a father to us but above all, it terrified me. I saw all the pitfalls it could bring given my strong tendency to affirm myself. The only thing that calmed me was what Garci told me, "Christ is placing this in front of you to make you more His."

1. World Youth Day in Madrid, August 2011

2. Cfr. Pope Benedict XVI, https://www.vatican.va/content/ benedict-xvi /en/homilies/ 2011/documents/hf_ben-xvi_hom_ 20110820_seminaristi-madrid.html, "Under the guidance of your formators, open your hearts to the light of the Lord, to see if this path which demands courage and authenticity is for you. Approach the priesthood only if you are firmly convinced that God is calling you to be his ministers, and if you are completely determined to exercise it in obedience to the Church's precepts."

3. Ignacio Carbajosa Pérez, diocesan priest and national leader of Communion and Liberation in Spain from 2010 to 2022.

RESPONSIBILITY

I started the year worried about my new responsibilities. Soon, my days were filled by appointments with people I was supposed to accompany, and I began to face my responsibility with anguish. Everything I did felt wrong. I couldn't please everyone and, on top of that, I was sad. I took on a burden that no one had asked me to carry and soon I started feeling physically sick. After several medical checkups, my parents (who had been saying it right from the start) showed me that it wasn't just a physical ailment—something was off.

On top of that, my relationship with Rocío really started to give me anxiety. I wanted to love her, but it was as if I couldn't—each time it became harder. My inability to be in the relationship became more and more evident, and at one point I told her about the worry, so as to figure out why I was loving her less when I wanted to love her more. We tried everything, talking more, talking less, praying more, praying less, but something still wasn't right. I blamed myself for our relationship going poorly. I started to live it as if the situation was my fault. I even remember talking to my uncle Yago and unloading on him with a huge rant about how my relationship with Rocío was failing because I hadn't worked on it hard enough. He corrected me, reminding me of everything we had been through.

Overwhelmed by everything (deep down, by my inability to make myself happy), I "cracked," and I let Rocío, my friends, and my parents know. I felt the urge to talk it over with Betty, and I wrote her perhaps the most honest email I've ever sent to anyone, "I'm doing poorly. I am sad and tired, and I don't know why." The very next day, I called her and we talked over Skype. I hadn't even finished my second sentence when I fell silent. While listening to me, she smiled and suddenly her gaze pierced right through me. She said, "Do you finally see that Christ is doing this because He prefers you, that this is His way of calling you?" Immediately I recognized this approach as His, I could see His face. The face of Christ, which I had already discovered, revealed itself a little more that day—like a blurry photo that gradually becomes clearer the longer you look at it. Once again, just like the first time it happened, silence and gratitude washed over me. It was like a huge weight was lifted my shoulders. I could finally breathe again. Rarely have I been able to perceive His face with the clarity I did in that moment. I vividly remember how recognizing Him required me to stop looking at myself for a moment and instead look at what was happening. Through Betty, yet again, that same face reached me and said, "Stop searching—I am here."

It's strange to look back at that moment as something that radically changed everything, and not some quick fix that spared me the journey or pain of facing what was happening with Rocío. Rather, it was as if it shifted my perspective, expanding my horizons and allowing a new possibility to emerge. Namely that it was Another calling me through these things, telling me that He wanted to be the one to bear the weight of my life. And so, through Betty's gaze, I began to live those days in constant dialogue with Him, moved by how insistently the Lord was calling me.

Yago and Garci were accompanying me closely during that period of time. Two weeks later, the situation with Rocío reached a critical point—I didn't know what to do. After talking with her about it, we decided it would be best for me to speak with Nacho and determine how to move forward. I remember calling Nacho in the morning and asking him, "What signs are there in a relationship to know whether to keep going or not?" I don't fully recall his response, but I do know that something welled up inside me that I didn't want to hear. A "no." And the truth is, a final verdict emerged within me with complete certainty, "The Lord is showing me this isn't it." I needed to let Rocío go. Stubbornly, I met up for lunch with one of my best friends, Igna, but again, the answer was no. Then that night I had dinner with someone who had been like a sister to me for a long time, Miras (I get emotional just thinking about these faces as true companions on the journey), and I remember her saying, "Marcos, I'm not going to tell you what to do, but I think deep down you already know." The Lord made it very clear what He wanted. The decision was in my hands. It was up to me as to whether I would follow the Lord or do my own will. Walking home with a broken heart, I surrendered to the facts. He was showing me what I had so often asked Him to reveal—His will. That same night, Rocío bombarded me with calls, and I had to tell her my decision over the phone, even before I could say it to her face. I remember her saying: "Okay, I'll pray for you. We'll see each other soon."

NOT GIVING UP ANYTHING

That weekend, before going to see Rocío in Pisa—she was on Erasmus in Florence that year—I spent time with Garci. By then, we were starting to see each other more often. I'd usually pick him up and take him to the airport each month when he came to Barcelona. Although we didn't know each other very well yet, one day, as I was dropping him off at the airport and we were saying goodbye, I sensed the same exceptional care that Christ had already shown me. He suggested we spend Christmas together and told me he wanted to accompany me more closely. That was a very significant moment for me. It came just a few days after making a decision I didn't want to make, grappling with a strong sense of contradiction and thinking that God had asked something of me that I didn't want, He showed me that He was with me. Through the tender companionship of José Miguel, God came to say, "I know you don't understand, but don't worry—I have you in the palm of my hand." I remember traveling to Pisa with a broken heart, but at peace, because the Lord had gone out of His way to prove He was taking close care of me.

On the plane, aware that I was about to do something I didn't want to do, an enormous sadness overwhelmed me, and I started thinking about what I truly desired—not what I felt like doing or what I would like to have happen, but what I genuinely longed for deep down. And I said to the Lord, "Alright, I trust You. Let Your will be done. But if I do this, You have to fulfill three requests. First, that my life becomes greater. Second, that Rocío's life becomes greater. Third, that our relationship, in whatever form You decide, lasts forever." Looking back now, I realize that the education I received from the movement (CL) was starting to sink in. I was taught not to give up on anything I desire. Giving up on Rocío, giving up on my love for her, would have been a defeat—a moment in my life that Christ didn't redeem, and thus it would have led me to doubt my faith. But I thought (taking into consideration everything I'd been told in CL), "When have I ever really lost anything? Do I have to renounce what I desire or deny it? No—if I entrust myself to the Lord, it's not to lose her, but to gain her." With this mindset, I went to see her. Now, looking back, I understand the heart of the matter. It wasn't so much about fighting against reality to make it bend the way I wanted, but about discerning what I truly desired, so I could marvel at how the Lord, with great creativity, fulfilled it.

Seeing her was one of the most painful things that has ever happened to me. To have the woman you love just a meter away and know that you cannot be unjust is difficult... You know you cannot tell her one thing and then do another. It was incredibly hard. I was dying to hug her or kiss her, but that would have confused everything and, ultimately, would have been much worse for her. It felt like a deep, wrenching tear. She was devastated, and I told her, "The Lord will accompany you, you'll see—He'll surely surprise you." It hurt so much that I had to call my uncle. I needed to know it was true, that the Lord would take care of her. And my uncle reassured me, "Don't worry—no one loves her like Christ does." That calmed me down.

The next day in class, I received a beautiful email from her in which she told me, with fascination, all the details of how the Lord had taken care of her through her friends in Florence. She shared the immense pain she was feeling, the thought haunting her that the Lord was taking everything away from her, but also how she recognized—something she hadn't acknowledged in a long time—that the Lord was spoiling her through the relationship she had with some of her friends. And she wrote, "I can't wait to see you, whenever God wills it, to tell each other what the Lord has done in us!" I'm still amazed by the love with which she accepted all of this and how much she respected my freedom until the very end. That "whenever God wills it" became our reference point for waiting. When will I see Rocío? When's the right moment? Simple. Whenever God wants, whenever He brings us together. It moved me to see that the Lord was beginning to fulfill what I desired in my relationship with Rocío.

THE RELATIONSHIP WITH HIM TAKES OFF

Suddenly, my relationship with the Lord took off—it began to take center stage in my life, and an overwhelming need for communion with Him started to grow within me. This led to nearly constant prayer and dialogue. Little by little, I began to feel a real call to virginity. It pained me that I had treated women the way that I had, it hurt to look at anything without keeping Christ in mind, and I started asking Him for that gift. I found myself falling in love with the hearts of my friends, with what was happening to them or what mattered to them. A deep desire emerged to accompany them as Christ would, and to look at them the way Christ does. I began to realize that it wasn't necessary to physically touch people (especially women) to convey affection or love. I became more interested in them discovering Christ than in them discovering me. In a very powerful way, a sense of fatherhood toward my friends began to take shape.

My life in general took off—in my relationships with my friends, with José Miguel, at university and in my studies, in reading, music, or movies, even in gazing at the clouds. Above all, a constant sense of gratitude and dialogue emerged in me.

In fact, looking back now, I realize that in my life, the things I liked and cared about weren't something I had to give up. I started enjoying everything even more. Even food! With Christ, everything gained a greater depth and flavor. The relationship with that mysterious "point" I had always experienced became even closer, and in the life of the Church, I lived that dialogue with increasing everyday awareness. Curiously, God continued to maintain all His mystery and remained beyond my understanding.

On top of that, listening to Carrón, I was blown away by something he said, "The vocation to virginity is a preference." That phrase stirred me deeply—the preference I longed for and had demanded of the Lord was being expressed in the vocation He was awakening in me.

More and more, certain relationships began to emerge in which I began to experience fatherhood, like with a girl named Yara. It's been a beautiful journey to discover that it wasn't me attracting people, but Christ—and that only by affirming Christ was I being true to those who approached me. I started to realize that the responsibility I was given for CLU, which Christ had asked of me, was a gift. What Garci had said was coming true. I was more His, because being in charge made me live and know the charism of CL in a way I never had before. I found myself falling in love again with the place where Christ called me. This is one of the most striking signs I am noticing as I walk this path, that I inevitably love the place where the Lord has put me more and better. Plus, it was a joy to have the friendships I had in the Diaconia and to see the journey we were all on together.

My relationship with my closest friends also took off, like with Igna, one of the most important people in my life. It's been beautiful to see how our loyalty to each other has grown and how we've helped one another find Christ. Or my relationship with Betta, or with the CLU in Barcelona, or those in Madrid, with whom a beautiful paternity is beginning. It's a remarkable gift to witness the journey others are on.

ARIZKUN

Then Christmastime arrived and I went to study for a week with Garci[1], who was becoming an authoritative figure in my life. I was the only one who would be with him during those days, and I remember thinking, "The Lord has even gone so far as to indulge my most childish desires, like allowing me to be preferred by him." The question of vocation was very alive in me at that time. Signs kept repeating themselves, like when a priest gave me the penance of reading a random Gospel passage, and I happened to land on the Solemnity of Jesus Christ, High and Eternal Priest. Around that time too, one night at dinner, my mother shared something with me that she never had before. She told me that at my baptism, the priest had entrusted me to the Virgin Mary to become a priest. That moment clarified so much about my childhood—like my relationship with women or that early sense of vocation—and I immediately started praying more and more to the Virgin Mary. On top of that, I was starting to feel a deep nostalgia for Rocío. Garci kept insisting, "Through this, Christ is teaching you to love as He loves."

That week changed my life. I spent the whole time watching Garci closely, paying attention to his gestures and the way he did things. I looked at him knowing that something great was happening in him too. Right away, I recognized myself as living the exact same experience as the disciples. I had the presence of Christ right before my eyes. Soon, Christ became the content of everything

1. Don José Miguel García and Marcos stayed for a week in the guesthouse of the Nuestra Señora de los Ángeles monastery in Arizkun (Navarra).

we did—when we talked, ate, studied, everything. The preference Garci showed for me, with immense tenderness, was the way God was telling me, "I have chosen you." My dialogue with Christ those days continued to grow in leaps and bounds. It became impossible not to ask myself, "Are You surprising me here too, Lord?" And little by little, the psalms we prayed throughout the day turned into pure poetry for me, the texts that best defined my life:

> Lord, you search me and know me, / you know when I sit or when I rise, / from afar you discern my thoughts, / you observe my path and my rest, / all my ways are familiar to you. / Where can I go from your spirit, / where can I flee from your gaze? / My days were determined / before the first one came.[2]

I never imagined just how real Christ really was. I began to belong to Him in a very profound way and to discover that, just like Garci, I wanted to depend on Him even more.

I remember landing in Barcelona and seeing my father tired from work and financial stress, and I said to him, "I'm sorry, Dad—whatever happens, and even though this hurts, it can't undo what's happened to me these past few days; it's too big."

From that point on, my relationship with Garci became much more intense. I shared everything happening in my life with him. Since then, he has become my father. Following Gius (Giussani) and following Christ means following him. I've embarked on a beautiful journey with him, growing more in my affection for Christ and affirming myself less. He has become the face Christ uses the most to accompany me closely, guiding and supporting me with great patience in my vocation. Whenever I hear him or others speak about Giussani's fatherhood, I think, "I'm living it too." More than a few times, he expressed that he desired and wanted to give his life for me. Never had it been so tangible to me that Christ gave His life for us on the cross. He often repeated to me, "My only desire is that you be dominated by awe at what Christ brings about."

2. Psalm 139.

It was very meaningful to me that he continually insisted that I am called to holiness. When I'd push back or object, he'd say, "Being a saint isn't about being perfect or consistent—it's about having a heart passionate for Christ."

At the leper colony in Calcutta

HOLY WEEK IN BENICASIM

During Holy Week, my family and Rocío's spent a few days together in Benicasim. I was already nervous in the days leading up to it. Since we parted, I had thought of her every day (especially when praying for her), and at times, it caused me a lot of pain. I remember in certain moments that the nostalgia I felt for her was so intense that I wanted to rip my heart out of my chest, shouting at the Lord, "Why are You doing this?" Seeing her was, just as I had imagined, very painful. But I had reasons to keep entrusting the relationship to God: my life had grown and hers, from what I could tell, had too. Plus, we looked at each other in a more beautiful way than we ever had when we were together. But the pain was overwhelming. The strongest I had ever felt.

It was in that moment that I understood in a very real way what Giussani meant when he spoke of virginity as the experience of being torn. I grasped the sacrifice he said was necessary for things to be true. He said, "Nothing is true without a sacrifice—nothing." When we finally talked (accompanied by our closest friends), it was impressive to see the immense good that the time spent apart and the form our relationship had taken had been for both of us, and even for our friends.

Everyone was grateful to be able to witness what we were living. At the time, I thought, "It's clear that all of this belongs to Christ, that it's for His glory." Moreover, I noticed the same signs of the Lord's preference in her life that I was experiencing. She also spoke about the need for silence, about how her dialogue with the

Lord had grown, and how she asked to depend more on Him. But the weeks following Holy Week were incredibly hard for me. I suffered more than ever before, feeling that the Lord was asking me for an enormous sacrifice without giving me an idea of what the final outcome would be (that's the best way I can put it). It became a deep pain that, at times, was a distraction. It also became an opportunity to offer my pain to Christ and to understand what His death on the cross meant for me. My uncle and Garci were a huge help during those days. They constantly encouraged me to revisit my reasons for accepting the Lord's will and letting go of Rocío. They spoke to me about their own experiences, helping me see that with time and through all the pain, things became more beautiful.

YOU HAVE GIVEN ME EVERYTHING

I saw Rocio again in the summer of 2012. We were in La Thuile at the CLU vacation[1]. It was the first time since Holy Week, and we agreed to talk. Sitting on one of the peaks of the Alps, with breathtaking views, we shared about each other's journeys and caught up. But we both did so with care, following the advice and guidelines Garci had given us to respect each other's path with discretion and to look at one another with virginity. I had prayed for that encounter for a long time, and it was one of the most beautiful things that has ever happened in my life. I remember at several points during the conversation, thinking with emotion, "Thank You." You could see in our eyes that our love for each other had multiplied. Our curiosity about each other's lives—studies, friendships—had tripled, and we were amazed at how genuinely interested we were in how the other was doing. And grateful, as if it were our own joy, for the good things happening to each other. It was a miracle to be able to speak freely about how difficult the journey had been and, at the same time, about how our relationship was helping us discover the Mystery at work. It hadn't been necessary to touch each other or explicitly declare our love to understand what had happened to us. We didn't need to possess one another—just to trust that Another would take care of our relationship as we followed our own path. For me, it was moving. The love we had for each other was true and beautiful. We had also accepted God's will for us.

1. In July 2012, Communion and Liberation university students (CLU) from the University of Milan and Spaniards organized a joint vacation in the alpine village of La Thuile.

I remember that as I was coming down the mountain, I was thinking about that moment on the plane and the three requests I had made to the Lord, completely overwhelmed by awe and immense gratitude. God has fulfilled everything I desired. He'd done it by giving me far more than I could have ever imagined. I remember saying to Him, "Lord, You've given me everything, everything—do with me as You wish, because I've discovered that with You, everything comes to fruition, that when I entrust something to You, You bring it to completion."

Remembering what happened during those days has become a source of joy for me. The nostalgia for Rocío is something that continually renews my relationship with God. She put it so well, "While everyone might say we're unfortunate, you and I know we're the preferred ones."

Now anytime doubts assail me, or when someone asks me if everything about Christ is true, all of this immediately comes to mind, and I think, "Impossible, I've seen it with my own eyes! Who else but Him is capable of something like this?" It's unthinkable to me that what happened with her was something I made happen, or that we somehow convinced ourselves of it. If that were the case, I never could have let her go. Seeing with my own eyes that after eight months of not speaking to the woman I love most, that both she and I love each other even more, is something otherworldly, something no one can make happen on their own. By following Christ, I don't love her less, but more. My faith is affirmed in what happened to me.

The path I am on has become, at its core, the greatest verification of my vocation. It is clear that I am called to virginity, because as soon as I let go of what I loved most and offered it to God, it turned into the most beautiful thing that has ever happened in my life. By following my vocation, Christ has fulfilled my life and Rocío's. He has made us look at each other in the way I have always longed to look and be looked at. That is how I discovered that this was the path the Lord was asking me to follow.

At times, I have been very impatient with my vocation. It surprises me how quickly the Lord has made me aware that this is my calling. Garci always told me, "For the Lord, there is no such thing as idle time. Everything happens for a reason." If the Lord wants me to live this time with greater awareness of my vocation, even though I will still need to wait a year or two before entering the Seminary, it's because He is "up to something," both with me and with those around me.

Because of everything that has happened, Christ will never cease to be real for me. This is especially true because of what He has done in my relationship with Rocío. There is a quote from C.S. Lewis that has really helped us,

> When I have learnt to love God better than my earthly dearest, I shall love my earthly dearest better than I do now. Insofar as I learn to love my earthly dearest at the expense of God and instead of God, I shall be moving toward the state in which I shall not love my earthly dearest at all. When first things are put first, second things are not suppressed but increased.[2]

In my story with Rocío, Christ has given me even more than I wished for, fulfilling what I desired.

2. Excerpt from a letter by C.S. Lewis to Mrs. Jacob, July 3, 1941.

THE LORD SHOWS ME THE NEXT STEP TO TAKE, HE WANTS EVERYTHING

"Amen, I say to you, there is no one who has given up house or brothers or sisters or mother or father or children or lands for my sake and for the sake of the Gospel who will not receive a hundred times more now in this present age: houses and brothers and sisters and mothers and children and lands, with persecutions, and eternal life in the age to come.[1]" Some time later, a great desire welled up in me for two things: first, to live life looking first at what is happening, really seeing what the Lord makes happen before my eyes; and second, to serve Him, to start thinking more about Him than about myself. Like José Miguel told me so many times, "to affirm Christ is to affirm yourself to the core." I still have a long way to go, but it has been beautiful to see what the Lord has brought about in some of my friends from University, like Paula or Adrián.

Furthermore, over the course of 2012, I made some progress. More than anything, life consisted in paying attention to what was happening and what was happening to me specifically, in order to understand what the Lord was trying to tell me in my daily life. One of the most interesting steps I took was entering into the habit of seeing life as a journey, a task. I'm much less afraid of being a constant "work in progress", meaning I am continuously trying to understand who I am and what is happening to me. The result is that I try to follow Him in everything that I do.

1. Mk 10, 29–30.

But more than anything, Christ is asking for a more loving and closer relationship with Him. In my relationship with Rocío, He has asked us to take a step further when it comes to the sacrifice we are making. The last few times we met that summer, she didn't want us to talk because it was hard on her. Garci proposed another important step, to sacrifice seeing her, looking at her, even thinking about her. Letting go has been very difficult. I thought I had already entrusted the entire relationship to God, that I was no longer possessive. However, in moments like this, He continues to show me that I am still attached to certain things (like talking to her). This latest separation has brought to light my need for affection. Something I never considered until now. Perhaps it's still related specifically to her. The Lord is asking for everything, for my entire life. He wants me for Himself, and only for Himself. He has taken hold of me and doesn't want to let go. And I want to find out if it's true, if I can live solely for Him and nothing else, because that means being truly and completely free.

Increasingly, I imagine the Lord (perhaps what I'm about to say might not be theologically sound) as a small, jealous child, wanting all my attention. He wants my heart and affection for Himself alone, calling me to a certain familiarity, to service, to a more profound rapport with Him. At the same time, He is also asking me to accept the sacrifices he demands so that I can become more united with Him.

I remember a conversation I had with Garci, a conversation that was very tough for me but very true. He told me, "There's a part of you that doesn't want to let go of Rocío. You will continue looking for gestures of affection from her, confirmation of her fondness for you. You have asked the Lord to make your relationship something eternal, but you've also formed an image of what that means. What if losing her is a sign from the Lord that He loves you?"

Those were days of immense pain, of continuous heartbreak, and even incomprehension. I thought a lot about St. Paul's phrase,

"I would glady give up everything to gain Christ.[2]" I resisted losing her, or at least fully and completely entrusting my relationship with her to the Lord. But my desire to say "yes" to Him was there. And with great pain, after begging the Lord to help me accept this "gladly," I finally did it. I remember looking at the painting of the Virgin Mary in my room with tears in my eyes and saying to her, "Yes, but it hurts; don't leave me alone." Finally letting go really cost me. I made it concrete by giving up seemingly trivial things like the photos I had of her or emails I reread nostalgically. Without being faithful and obedient to every suggestion the Lord made to me, nothing in my life would remain alive and lasting. At that specific moment in my life and Rocío's as well, the Lord was asking us to really distance ourselves from one another. We needed enough space to allow us to embrace our vocation.

I am amazed at how quickly the Lord showed me that He was with me. He knew that this decision—which I also knew was for the best—was painful, but He did not leave me alone. Even though at first it was hard to understand, the idea that the Lord was asking for all of me was an unthinkable act of His preference for me. By making me more His, he was "taking away" what was still not fully rooted in Him, the One that is my only true destiny. At the same time, He was purifying everything and making it new, including a more beautiful and true relationship with Rocío. Indeed, the Lord immediately showed me that He was with me. The next day, during charitable work, the nuns at the soup kitchen[3] asked me to read the Gospel (in the kitchen, before serving, it is read) four times (once for each shift). After spending two days crying in corners, the Sisters of Calcutta had me read--four times--the Gospel in which Christ says to the mother who has lost her son, "Woman, do not weep.[4]" One cannot imagine what it was to hear

2. Marcos is referring to Phil 3, 8–10

3. Marcos regularly volunteered at the soup kitchen of the Missionaries of Charity in Barcelona.

4. Lk 7,13

and see how God was willing to bend down over my nothingness to embrace me.

Excursion with friends from the CLU of Barcelona

AN EVEN GREATER VOCATION, AN EVEN GREATER EVERYTHING: THE *VERIFICA*[1]

And once again, life is multiplied a hundredfold. Everything becomes more beautiful, more intense. One cannot imagine how it's possible to be happier, but then you are. That is how studying, the school of community, a conversation, a message, washing dishes, a backache, sadness, a sacrifice, exercising, watching the clouds or a beautiful woman, or even my sin—all become opportunities to renew my relationship with Him. As R. Guardini says, "In the experience of a great love, all that happens becomes an event inside that love.[2]" Everything becomes vocation, everything becomes the way in which Another chooses to educate you, makes you grow, restores your awareness, and tells you that He is with you and loves you. Only with Christ do I perceive that my reason is increasingly open to recognizing everything He gives me without taking it for granted.

And that's how I have come to rediscover the immense preference that the Lord has for me. Living the paternity He calls me to live, or participating in the CLU, just like in other activities, has become the joy of my life, the meaning of my life, the way to tell the world that I know Christ and that He makes me happy.

1. Verifica (in Spanish, "grupo de verificación") consists of a series of meetings for young people who want to verify and discern their vocation to God in virginity.

2. Romano Guardini, The Essence of Christianity.

This implies a different perspective on everything—toward women, studies, trees, or a beautiful landscape, family, my own mistakes or those of others. Life with Him changes you so much that one even begins to become a child in front of what happens to oneself. You find yourself surprised by an interaction, a certain conviction, or the gaze of another that leaves you in awe and compels you to acknowledge that Another is present.

Starting the *verifica* has been yet another sign of this. There is a place designed specifically for me, where there are people who share the same call from the Lord. There is a place ready to educate me to live always more amazed by what He does. It is a place that welcomes me as I am and cares about serving and helping me through whatever is happening to me. A true miracle. In this new life I am living, I find myself saying very often, "This has changed my life," "I hope I say this all my life!"

Throughout the *verifica*, I've been amazed to see how, day by day, the Lord is present in my life and calls me to the vocation of virginity. In one of the *verifica* lessons, Giussani provides two criteria to discern if the intuition of being called to a life of virginity is true. I was struck by how his criteria confirm and explain my own experience. The first is an increase in the joy of living in the present. How many times have I caught myself saying, "How is it possible that suddenly the university, friendships, and all of life have become so beautiful just by following this intuition!" The second involves adopting Christ's criteria, His concerns as my own. For example, love for the Church, for the movement, and for sharing the pain of the Church when it is not true to itself or when one of its members—or a friend in the movement—goes astray.

I never cease to thank the Lord for granting me the grace to experience the *verifica*, and to do it with Prades[3], a true father who, before any objection, complaint, or difficulty has always insisted on love for the person of Christ. He has urged us to live by discovering whether or not our relationship with Him corresponds

3. Fr. Javier Prades, diocesan priest of Madrid.

to our heart. He has helped me to face the sacrifices we're asked by telling us, "If you don't encounter the loving initiative of Another in your life, it's impossible to give Him your life. Curiously, one can only give everything when one has everything." The *verifica* is a precious gift from the Lord, and I'm grateful He has granted me the grace to go through it with two of my friends, Aida and Lucía.

With Yago, Marc, and José Miguel in Jerusalem

A STEP FORWARD IN MY RELATIONSHIP WITH GARCI; A STEP FORWARD IN MY INTIMACY WITH CHRIST

Little by little, the greatness of my friendship with José Miguel, which Christ has generated and is deepening, has introduced the intuition and desire that it also be a unique relationship, an increasingly all-encompassing preference, where both he and I give our lives for one another. Garci has always been very aware of this preference. More than once he insisted that he saw our friendship as the place where Christ preferred to enter into his life, and therefore as something sacred that we must nurture and for which we must constantly pray.

It has been astonishing to see how this friendship has gradually encompassed everything in our lives, to the point of sharing everything, even money. Little by little, as I constantly verify that he is the most authoritative person the Lord has placed in my life, I have tried to be even more present in our relationship and to take care of him too. The desire has grown to be like Christ in his life and to accompany him in the way that Christ desires. I will be grateful my whole life for what has happened with him: It has introduced me in a remarkable way to the love of Christ for myself and for others—all in a very simple way—by loving me. The relationship with José Miguel and the desire for a holy friendship, rooted in the Lord, extend into my relationship with Christ. More and more, our friendship is a sign of His Presence. Being with him, talking with him, or thinking of him is being with Christ, talking with Christ, or thinking of Christ. This is how tangible He becomes in our lives!

THE RELATIONSHIP WITH ROCÍO, A STEP TOWARD MATURITY

Eventually I saw Rocío again during a study weekend in Madrid. We talked about our lives and about Christ. I was struck by how she is increasingly a sign for me: I am moved by seeing her, even thinking about her, by the fact that she exists. For the first time since we parted ways, we could look at each other and say that we love each other, that we miss each other, and that we pray for one another every day—all without a single hint of ambiguity. What a grace! That weekend, for the first time in my relationship with her, I desired for Him to be more present than myself. In truth, it wasn't the first time. I have vaguely intuited and desired that before, but it was the first time it came to me with absolute clarity. I wanted the time we spent and conversation we had together to make her thank and love Christ more than me. It is thrilling to grow little by little in the desire to be identified with Christ, and a miracle to see how He makes it happen.

It also became clearer than ever that she is not mine. It wasn't easy to accept that I am not the center of her life, but I had to admit that, in truth, I never had been the center. In that moment, it was evident that I possessed her less. Likewise, I realized that the people God has chosen for this moment in her life are other people and no longer me. It reminded me that sacrifice is something constantly renewed and that it is necessary to decide again and again, to surrender her to God with total resolve.

Singing on the mountain with friends

CHRIST, AN UNMISTAKABLE, PERSONAL FACE

I want to emphasize here that, even though it may sound strange to say, Jesus has a unique, personal face. He has a face that does not coincide with our own. He makes use of our face, but His is a unique face. The person of Jesus has His own personal gaze. After every encounter in my life, I have not stopped growing in this awareness. In other words, I continue to grow in the awareness that it is important to speak of Him, and that this is not speaking of just anything or anyone, but of a unique person with His own personality.

Affection for Christ is affection for His person, the same one the disciples knew or whom the Virgin carried in her womb. It is in my affection for Him that I increasingly give thanks for everything, my affection for the One that I increasingly understand to be Everything.

At this point, I want to highlight how crucial it has been to follow Carrón and, through him, Giussani. As Giussani says, "Without a tender gaze toward ourselves, it is as if there were no solid ground on which to build.[1]" This work of self-awareness, of

1. Julián Carrón Pérez, Has anyone ever promised us anything? Then why should we expect anything? CLU Spiritual Exercises, Traces 2012, pg. 11 "'Affection for oneself, says Fr. Giussani, is an "attachment full of esteem and compassion, of mercy, for oneself [...]. It's like having for oneself a bit of that attachment that your mother had for you, especially when you were little." Imagine the tenderness with which a mother holds her newborn in her arms, moved by the very existence of that child, aware of all the desire for happiness that will be unleashed in him, through the great destiny to which he is called. If there is not a bit of this tenderness in us, of this affection for ourselves, continues Fr. Giussani, "we lack the ground upon which to build."'

realizing what I am, the infinite value of our self, and the fact of having been created, is something I am becoming more familiar with and that is helping me to have a more tender and merciful gaze on myself. All of the judgments that Carrón spoke about during the Spiritual Exercises of the CL University Students were embodied in Garci, who always looks at me with tenderness, seeing me for who I am, without having to ignore any of my sin or nothingness. Now, thanks to God, I realize that my "measure" is not the true measure of who I am. Christ is the only true measure; His criterion is the true and final criterion. I am a perpetual gift. I am a permanent gift that He gives me, for I am nothing and I need Him in everything I do.

RESPONSIBILITY, SERVICE AND FREEDOM

Throughout the year[1], it has become clear to me just how much the Lord has made use of the responsibility He entrusted to me with the CLU. Some of my friends have gone through difficult moments, struggling to follow the movement. On occasion, I have had a tough decision to make, an action to correct or a suggestion to make that the recipient might not appreciate. It has been beautiful to discover how Christ, through these situations, asks me, "Do you choose Me or yourself?" He has challenged me again to consider what my value is, what defines me. The question is whether to follow Jesus and affirm Him or to worry about myself and how I appear. God has made me grow in freedom through what has happened in the CLU, especially in difficult situations. During the year, even when some of my friends offended me or others in the community, I have kept repeating the following, "If you are in Christ, if you are in the truth, a tender gaze toward them will emerge." So, when I didn't find this gaze in myself, I recognized that something was wrong, that I was focusing on something else instead of keeping my attention on Him. Moreover, realizing what gives you life when things get tough is a joy that overcomes any circumstance, no matter how arid or painful it might be.

I am continually conquered by this Love, by this face, by this presence, by Jesus Christ. This phrase from Fr. Giussani never ceases to amaze me, "Christ who begs for man's heart, and man's

1. 2014

heart that begs for Christ."[2] I also want to live for Him. I want to live for Him who died for me, who communicates his life to me from His Cross. I want to serve Him and give my life for Him. Looking at my life, I realize that I have always chosen—or rather, discovered—what I desire. I have always strived to discover who I am. Now it is Christ who has decided the form this gift will take. He has given this gift to me, and by doing so, he has also fulfilled my desire. I am pleased to see how it is being fulfilled, to see that my life is an adventure, and that I am happy.

Marcos Pou

2. Speech given by Msgr. Luigi Giussani during the meeting of the Holy Father John Paul II with Catholic movements and new communities. Luigi Giussani, Javier Prades López, Stefano Alberto, *Generating Traces in the History of the World*, McGill-Queen's University Press 2010.

At Jordi and Silvia's Wedding

www.ingramcontent.com/pod-product-compliance
Lightning Source LLC
LaVergne TN
LVHW051015080826
845145LV00009B/2627